Seek Joy

Find Beauty, Share Love

Saira Priest

For Mummy with Love

About This Book

If you let them, flowers can hold great messages for us. Words we need to hear, usually words we already know and would like to be confirmed by a friend. Flowers can be those friends who tell us what we want to hear, show us what we need to see, and allow us to love what we feel. Each time we allow it, we learn a little bit more about our true selves and our nature. We get closer to our authentic beings.

This book is designed to slow down the busy-ness of life and allow us to get quiet, to find peace of mind, return to center, to rejuvenate, to let go what we need to and build courage and resolve for the things we must, and indeed, want to do. This book can be read before, after or as a meditation. It helps to arrive at the present moment to see where you are. Insights will be revealed to you.

Relax and leaf through the pages casually to calm the mind. See which flowers and words draw you in easily. Which ones move you? Where do you feel resistance? Why? Which ones delight you? What does that tell you? Take time to look at the flowers which speak to you the most and see what secrets they hold for you.

Seek Joy

All the answers are in nature.

"If we could see the miracle of a single flower clearly, our whole life would change."

Buddha

Slow down to find the jewel.

Just Sit.

Care to Serve

Care to serve others? We are better able to serve others when we have first cared for ourselves and are as strong as we can be. Gently attend first to your needs. Ask your body what it needs. Is your throat dry? Refresh it with a tall glass of water. Begin the flow. Did your belly grumble or do you feel yourself slowing down, feeling weak or shaky? Energize with an apple, an orange, some grapes, pineapple or crunch on some carrots. Perhaps a cup of yogurt or a handful of nuts sounds better. Re-charge. Energize.

Has your bladder tried to get your attention a couple of times now? Release the toxins. Free the flow. Feeling a little tense? Take a full breath in and release completely. Repeat. Make room for your inner light to glow outward. Begin now with simple, basic steps. Each day, listen to your body. Only *you* can take care of *you* best.

Allow

The Process

Every thought is a seed

Each thought we think is a seed, a groundwork laid for a future garden of thoughts, feelings, words and actions. It is said that we create our own reality. We may get an inkling, a gift of opportunity from infinite source. Then our free will offers us choice in thought. Human creation begins with a thought. This implies proactive choice in thought, which leads to emotion, and further to either more thought, conversation, behavior or deed. Some may not have considered the genesis of a thought as a choice, inasmuch as we sometimes refer to the resulting feelings without empowerment. That we can even think about this, tells us that we can choose.

As thoughts affect feelings, then do we not also choose our feelings, secondarily, as we laid the seeds for those in our past thoughts? Indeed, our purest and perhaps only real power lies in choosing our thoughts, thoughts which reflect our attitude and our perspective, which ultimately form our character.

Like choosing wisely that with which we nourish our bodies, we, too, can choose to select the thoughts with which we nourish our minds, our feelings, and in turn our bodies - and ultimately - our souls. What seeds shall we choose to plant today for tomorrow's desired bountiful harvest?

Grow inside while ice has ceased your movements.

**Between the Bud and the Beauty,
much unfurling takes place.**

Be there.

Relax. Meditation is just practice.

When we approach life with the thought that there need not be high pressure "moments of truth" in which we must perform perfectly, we see that all of life is just practice. Each moment in life is just practice for the next moment. Each moment we are fully present and give it our all, we feel momentarily complete. Each moment we are focused elsewhere outside of the present moment, we will have another chance to form a different habit. Another chance to practice to be more fully present.

Life is like this, it keeps returning opportunities to us again and again, until we get it "right". "Right" meaning that we are fully present and fully attentive to the moment as we wish it to be. Such that if we wish a moment had gone better, it is okay, because we will once again have another chance to practice again. Through practice, we keep the lightness and fullness of each moment in itself. Life is the practice. In this way, all of life can be meditation.

All is well, all is Zen.

Each moment is just practice

**Face Fear.
Question Fear.
Is it true?**

Acknowledge Pain

Watch it s o f t e n

You are right where you are supposed to be.

Sometimes in life, we find ourselves filled with regrets of the past and anxious about the future. All we have is this moment. Each moment lived with joy creates a tomorrow of satisfaction and yesterdays of positive reflection. We begin now. Just do the next joyful thing. Now. We all know that joy and happiness is found, created and felt in the present moment. How do we apply that to our life? How do we become present in this moment? We take a deep breath in, let it go and smile! Keep breathing with lungfuls of smiles. Remember, you can do nothing of the past - no one else can either.

The future is just made up of moments of now. Create a brighter future, simply by finding joy in each moment of now. Whoever you are, wherever you are - <u>it is right where you are supposed to be</u> and *you* are who *you* are supposed to be. Nothing more. Nothing less. You have been given your breath of life - take it in fully and live each moment with the gratitude of each moment. Begin now - with a smile!

Reflect

Connect

A Don Henley song is running through my head, "I think it's about forgiveness." It *is* about forgiveness. First and foremost, it is about forgiveness of self. I spoke with a new neighbor today and he shared with me the loss of his 18 month old son. He lost him 10 years ago. Yet I could hear the burden of his pain in his voice and this need to share with a stranger. Of course, the loss of a child is one of the most difficult things to experience. One of the struggles to deal with seems to be the aspect of forgiveness of self - forgiving ourselves lovingly - no matter what sins we feel we may have committed. Letting go of the baggage of self-imposed guilt (*all* guilt is self-imposed - it is empowering to know, because we have the power to let it go), energizes us to be free to serve our purpose on earth and to be of greater service to others.

Be very gentle in your forgiveness of yourself - treat yourself as you are - an innocent young child who did not know better, one who meant no harm, or simply had been led astray. Forgive yourself, forgive others - all others - and be the child in you. Returning to your path, to whom you know, your center, is simply choosing this moment and beginning now. Every now is a new beginning. Fill your lungs with a long fresh breath of air, fully release, with another full breath, smile and be who you are, innocence renewed. Begin now.

"I think it's about forgiveness"

Unfurling . . .

. . . each of us.

Rise

for

Sunrise

Love your life - every bit of it. Find every ounce of reason and shower it with the gratitude you truly feel for each ounce. Sometimes we are offered perspective by an incident in our own lives through an illness, an inconvenient house repair, etc. to remind us how good our lives had been up until that point. Sometimes, a tragedy elsewhere, such as an earthquake in Haiti, a flood in Mexico, a fire in a forest, occurs to remind us of what exactly and oftentimes, more, that we have taken for granted.

With ample and daily living in gratitude - and treasuring this incredible gift of life we have been given, we are better able to offer ourselves, our own gifts, our own gratitude, and our own help to those who are suffering. Love your life! Loving our own gift of life to the fullest is the simplest way to serve others.

Love Your Life!

What are you seeking?

Deeply ponder this question. Take your time, over the next few minutes, hours, months, however long. Keep asking and answering this question.

What am I really seeking?

What is the fluid that will fill my vessel. Is it wealth, fame, power? Is it a bigger house, more stuff? If I get those things, then will I be happy? Will I feel fulfilled?

Be

Is it happiness itself I seek? What is the definition of happiness in my life? Write down words that attract you - that you like the sound of, or that you like to say - within this context. Keep asking. Keep thinking. Keep breathing deeply as you ask. Keep observing and listening.
Take note of your answers. Ask again. Listen.

Life is a maze - have fun!

Walk effortlessly through life as if in a maze.

Every block eliminates a possibility and gets you another step closer to the light.

Taking the bad with the good

There is a causality and a reason for everything.
There is no good and bad, things just are as they are.
People have formed a thought pattern of distinguishing one from the other for the sake of safety.

As human tendencies go, so it is that some of us walk through life viewing all as bad and forgetting to look at what can be the good, even within the bad. Some of us look only at the good and pretend that the bad does not exist, shunning it, as though it had no place in life.

Within the whole lies a happy middle ground.

In marriage, "for better or worse" - what does such a vow infer? The "better" is probably easier to define, and we always have the choice to choose the focus on the "better". - The "better" attributes of the other that would outshine the "worse" attributes, which we also must accept within ourselves.

And the "worse" is often that attribute within ourselves which we reflect upon the other. So we are accepting of the "worse" of our spouse's reflections, as we want acceptance for our own attributes, again knowing that the "better" or good outshines, and will, always. As long as we accept both, take in the whole, emphasize the "better" and continue to work on individual growth, we will find a balance - the happy middle ground.

There is a saying, "That which we resist, persists." What does that mean to you? Personally. When walking through your day, any day, when approaching someone, stranger or known, deeply loved individual or otherwise. What makes you want to take flight? Consider how you feel when approaching a place, a task. Where in your body do you feel the weight of that resistance? Explore what it is telling you. If you faced it, what would happen? Could it be possible that something you desire resides within that resistance? And what if you approached it with a perspective opposite of what is usual or normal? What do we run from? Do we want it to persist? What do we want to run to? Whatever created the persistence holds the secret to freeing the resistance. That secret lies in you. Explore it and walk towards it with open arms.

"The hurt you embrace becomes joy.
    Call it to your arms where it can change."   Rumi

Quieting
the noise.

We all know that to find peace of mind and purpose, we need to find our center of calm. My father taught us to always look for the meaning in everything. Often I find that there is much noise to be filtered to find the gem, the kernel of truth. In seeking truth, we will have to quiet the noise. By doing this, we hear only those messages that are for us. Seek out tools and resources. For centuries, sages from all walks of life have and continue to seek this sanctuary. Many have found answers and have shared them. Seek these out. Go towards that which draws you closer to your center.

Let your LOVE shine.

Permission for Joy

When our son was born, the most valuable gift (in addition to the child) that we received was a plain card passed forward from another mother who had received this blessing. The inscription simply read:

" If Mama's Happy, Everybody's Happy."

This gift was treasured because it was from a harmonious household. It took much reflection over this phrase to realize that too often, too many of us take responsibility for others' happiness, and turn over the responsibility for our own to others' hands. Permission for joy, first for herself, gives permission to others to do the same - and is every mother's honor, opportunity and way to turn a house into a joyful home. When I receive the love which is in my heart into my own hands - then outward - true happiness and harmony are the rewards.

With joyful gratitude, taste happy!

Find Beauty

Hope.

Plant seeds of happiness

Seeds of positive intent are like a garden of flowers blooming in a profusion of colors and fragrance. What are weeds? Plants we would not choose to grow in our garden. Thoughts are like this too. Thoughts of negativity are seeds of weeds.

Positive thoughts are flowers we choose to grow. Sowing the seeds of either takes the same effort, energy, and proper conditions to grow. We have only to exercise our freedom of choice in our seed selection process. We choose our thoughts, which determine our intent, which flows through our actions, and is returned back to us (karma, luck, etc.). We always have the choice of a pleasant thought. What do you choose? I choose happy.

Faith

Trust

Trust in yourself, trust in the universe

Trust, trust, trust. Trust first in yourself, for you have immense powers. Trust in your powers, for they are meant for only good intentions. Trust next in your intentions, they are there for good reason. Trust in your choices.

You made decisions with good intentions and reasons of the moment. Trust in each moment. Trust next in your desire to do good. Trust, then, the universe for honoring that desire to do good. Trust in the future. Trust next in your fellow man and woman, for each desires to do their own good. Trust, too, in the universe to honor their good. Trust in the seasons. Trust in nature. Trust in time. Trust in this very moment that everything will be all right. Trust that everything already is all right. Trust in yourself. Trust in powers greater than yourself. Trust, trust, trust.

Only YOU can tell YOUR story.

Your story can only be told by you. I read somewhere that if you don't tell your story, nobody else will. The truth is that even if others might get the urge or try to tell your story, only your telling of it makes it truly your story. How many beautiful stories have we read that have touched our hearts, opened our minds, affected our emotions, moved our spirits. The courage of those writers allowed us a glimpse into our own humanity and of our universal connectedness to all things. We each have a story inside us, every one of us, and it is up to us to tell our own. Our life is our story. Begin today by writing just one page, one paragraph, one sentence, even just one word. We can begin anywhere, there is no magic formula or perfect place or best way. Simply begin with a memory, a feeling, a thought about our life right now, a hope for the future. Your story is worth sharing. Share it with someone today - that someone could be yourself.

You have always belonged

Inhale . . .

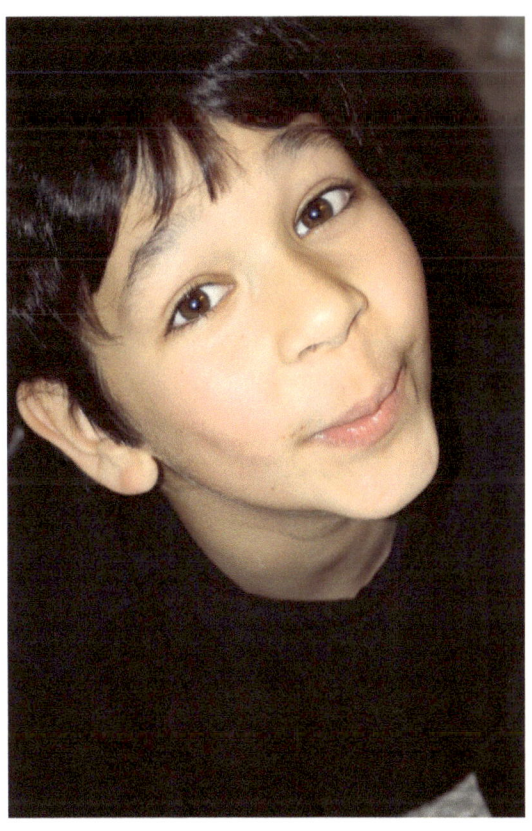

. . . Exhale

Recently, when asked why I always forgive - being caught unaware that forgiveness could be viewed as something to defend - my off-guard answer was probably something like, "What are the alternatives?" Upon reflection, I would have preferred to say that when I forgive, I allow the healing of wounds inside of me. Healing the wounds allows me to return to my center, the place of pure love, the place we like to be.

I guess it takes such reminders to help us remember the ebb and flow of life. The ebb being wound-causing and healing and the flow being returning to self through reflection and beginning again, and ultimately leading us to exercise the one choice we always have. The option only we can apply on our own selves, and that is, given the ever-present choice to have a positive outlook, choosing forgiveness of others and ourselves gets us to our center quickly and gently. So I can return to being at peace with myself, in a state of love - I guess that is why I always forgive.

Remembering the ebb and the *flow*

Hug

There's room for everyone

Smile at each other

Do your dance

Reach
for the sky, the sun

Reach for help. First reach in. Deeper inward. See the light. Deeper still. Allow the light to illuminate the help you seek until it has a clear definition. Fill yourself with intent to seek such help. Now begin to reach out. See more light. Now up. Fill yourself with this light in all its colors. Now in front and to each side. Lean back. Pay attention. Without assigning, see the help as it arrives, in any form. Receive the help. For in receiving, you are also giving.

Bloom

In Tandem

Gently

Focus *See Beauty Within* *Wait*

Gratitude

Savor the Nectar

Glow

Take Turns

Share Love

How to be happy

"*Even for our own happiness, even for our own survival, compassion is the most important factor. It is the most precious thing, more precious than all the wealth in the world. The good heart is more important than friends, lovers, wealth, fame, or anything else. Practicing the good heart is more important than all other forms of education. Practicing the good heart is the most important form of meditation. The good heart makes your whole life beneficial.*"
Lama Zopa Rinpoche

In Unity

Join

You already have maximum security

Once emerged, a butterfly arms itself with only its purpose.

I received a telemarketing call from a company offering "maximum security." I wondered what maximum security would look like.

Then there was an 80+ year old lady who armed herself with many self-perceived methods of safety from dangers she was convinced might cause her harm. When the time came for her soul to leave her body, none of those methods were of any use. And so it is that we spend much of our lives protecting ourselves either from past harms, future fears, or harms that may have occurred to others but will never happen to us. Then what do we have control over?

Our true and only security resides in how we choose to view and live life, which is the greater power, indeed. When we ask ourselves, what are we protecting ourselves from, really? When the clear answers reveal themselves, they surprise us, especially when we realize that the shields we have been holding up have kept us from the very thing we actually seek. We seek Love. Maximum security comes from love - only love and in just being loving and open to love. We already have love in one form or another, for love always shows up. We are love. We have always been love.

Dream **BIG**

Believe

Feel from the bottom of your heart

What is your purest intention?

Live Your Life!

In Australia, the Aboriginal tribes have a saying that goes something like, "Your life is your story, so make it a great story!" A story worth telling. A story of a life well lived. What is a good story for you? How do we live it? To do that, we must do something really good to and for ourselves.

Today, this week, this month or this year, take that adventure you always wanted, visit the place of your dreams, call someone you have been thinking about, join that club, paint that picture, play that sport, read that book, take that class, fulfill a dream, spend a day in the park with your child, cook that fancy dish that you are saving for a special occasion.   Today is the special occasion for which we have been saving everything. Each new day we are given is that special day. Start with today, live your story, write your life!

Make Your Story Great!

"...the sacred is in the ordinary
... everything is miraculous."

Abraham Maslow

"There is a soul force in the universe,which, if we permit it, will flow through us and produce miraculous results."

Gandhi

We get so many messages to process throughout the day from myriad sources that really affect how our moments are lived and felt. Which ones do we discard and which ones do we retain? We get to choose. We can train ourselves through the act of choosing which ones nurture us and help us grow. As we learn to hear and teach ourselves more of these types of messages with each breath, I am peace, I am joy, I am love. . . we begin to feel the power of the positive mantras as they release energy in our bodies and in our minds, arising from our limitless source of spirit. I am inspiration. When needing an initial boost, look first to this limitless source inside. Remind and invoke that which you seek, I am peace, I am joy, I am love.

I am peace, I am joy, I am love . . .

Look up

Lead

Love: the ever-present choice

When faced with any kind of confusion or indecision, it helps to keep in mind the one thing we have control over: the choice of our thoughts - which lead to our outlook, viewpoint, perspective, our attitude towards a given situation. Within all of that, there is the ever-present choice of choosing the love perspective. Love, after all, is the essence of all life.

Love is what we are trying to reconnect to, or to return to, or to maintain being in. We all have varying degrees of a taste of love at some point(s) in our past - even moments of such intensity that we can vividly recall the way the earth felt when we were in that light. Remember the light. Just the light. Remember the essence. Being there, all else is just noise. All else falls away, naturally, when we choose love.

"Let us keep this truth before us.

You say you have no faith?
  Love - and faith will come.

You say you are sad?
  Love - and joy will come.

You say you are alone?
  Love - and you will break out of your solitude.

You say you are in hell?
  Love - and you will find yourself in heaven.

Heaven is Love."

Carlo Carretto

Open Heart

Sweet Surrender

Love Is The Great Truth

"Love is a symbol of eternity.

It wipes out all sense of time,

destroying all memory of a beginning

and all fear of an end."

Writer and Photographer
Saira Priest

Spreading joy through images of nature's beauty and writing.

Also look for her other books found on Amazon:

Zen of Hoarding
http://www.zenofhoarding.com

and

If We Were…
(a children's book)

Connect with her online:

twitter: @sairapriest

www.sairapriest.com

Appreciation

Thank you for reading and sharing this book!

Spread Joy

Please support our authors by writing reviews on Amazon!

Seek Joy, Find Beauty, Share Love
Author & Photographer: Saira Priest
copyright 2013 - all rights reserved
Niche Publishing & Marketing
ISBN: 978-0-9726628-2-0
inspirational, photography, nature, meditative
www.sairapriest.com www.nichepublishing.US